# The Accidental Caregiver's Survival Guide

## Your Roadmap to Caregiving Without Regret

# A. Michael Bloom

MA, MS, CPC

**Limits of Liability and Disclaimer of Warranty**

**Warning – Disclaimer**

Cover design by Local Kid Productions

ISBN: 978-0-9897573-1-7

# About the Author

Burnout, stress, and overwhelm can lead to very undesirable consequences for caregivers, families, and organizations. Since 2011, Certified Professional Coach and Energy Leadership™ Master Practitioner Michael Bloom has helped to revitalize the careers of hundreds of family and professional caregivers with practical, tactical, soul-saving coping strategies, supporting them in saving lives. With a wealth of practical expertise as both a family and professional caregiver, Michael serves as a welcome and sought-after catalyst to guide caregivers and health and human services leaders to stay energized and committed to work that has never been more important or vital than it is today. Having earned two Master's Degrees in Psychology and Social Policy, Michael's passion for lifelong learning is best expressed through the practical sharing of game-changing tips that make urgent and real impact when and where they are needed most.

Whether you work with Michael in a private mentoring program, choose emergency roadside assistance coaching, or engage with him in one of his compelling and practical group workshops, you are sure to immediately recharge your energy and take inspired action towards to achieving the life of abundance and joy that you so richly deserve.

Happy clients say many remarkable things about the impact of Michael's work on their lives and work. This comment speaks volumes:

*"Michael Bloom is like a warm chocolate chip cookie that offers the delight and perks of comfort food without the calories."*
~ Sandy Putnam-Franklin

Take the immediate temperature on your level of burnout risk by taking a *free* Caregiving Burnout Risk Assessment!

By taking this complimentary assessment, you will:

1. Quickly and easily determine your caregiving stress factors.

2. Reveal what is draining your burnout-busting reservoirs and leaving you in a constant state of concern and worry.

3. Lay the foundation for areas of development to start living your own fulfilling life as a caregiver.

4. Kickoff your journey to caregiving without regret.

Go to www.BurnoutRisk.com and register for *free* access to complete "Your Caregiving Burnout Risk Assessment." It is very easy and quick to complete!

# Dedication

This book is dedicated to my parents, Irving and Berneice Bloom, affectionately known as Sonny and Bunny to those who loved them.

Mom and Dad, there is not a day that passes without my admiration and gratitude for all you accomplished in life and provided for me. Each and every step of our journey together was an adventure filled with exploration, learning, and love. Although you have passed on to the next life, I carry you with me and strive every day to honor your legacy in support to others.

My greatest transformational journey began during my care for you in your elder years. My first essay to be published about our experiences together appeared in the 2013 Edition of *The Gratitude Book Project*. This published essay (shared below) served as the impetus for writing this book.

# Parent Caregiving Without Regret

I am grateful that both of my parents were able to age in place and die with dignity in the comfort of their home. My father passed away in December of 2009 and my mother on Mother's Day 2012 – both in my loving arms as they drew their last breaths.

For three years, I had the most challenging and soul-fulfilling journey of my life. I served as the primary live-in caregiver for my parents, Irving and Berneice. In August of 2009, my then 82- year-old father suffered catastrophic heart failure. Prior to that event, he served as my mother's primary caregiver after her survival from Stage 4B Hodgkin's disease left her frail and in need of his physical support. My father's heart failure led to vascular dementia and the need for his own 24-hour care, so I stepped in to support them both.

During this personal and profound caregiving journey, I took care of the most intimate of hygiene routines and navigated the healthcare system for needed adaptive equipment, assistance, and respite support. Although still grieving, I am filled with gratitude that I returned all of the unconditional love and support ever shown to me without one moment of regret.

# Acknowledgements

*When you feel weak, ill, sad, or exhausted, do not hesitate to reach out to others for help. Don't keep bulldozing or fighting your way through until you crash or pass out. Apply the oxygen mask of loving support to yourself and breathe in the energy, healing, and inspiration of others. You will feel so much better for it in more ways than one.*

~ A. Michael Bloom

Thank you to all of the special family members and friends that I am blessed to have in my life. Your energy and support gave me the oxygen to carry on through the most challenging of times. Your admiration, cheerfulness, and love give me the boost to move forward with brilliance and intention.

Thank you to the many collaborators, colleagues, mentors, and teachers who are helping me to fully live my mission and reach more caregivers who are in desperate need of practical coping strategies to do work that has never been more important or vital than it is today. There are far too many to name individually but know that I admire and appreciate each and every one of you. I am especially grateful for choosing to pursue certification in professional coaching from the most comprehensive and personally transformative training program at iPEC (The Institute for Professional Excellence in Coaching).

Thank you to the dedicated caregivers who give selflessly to support their loved ones. You are part of the greatest caring force of humanity. It has been a great honor to coach many special caregivers in a partnership of mutual learning, growth, and development as they created more fulfilling lives for themselves and those they care for.

Thank you to each and every caregiver who is reading this book in order to get off "Caregiver Isolation Island" to seek the desired resources to serve their loved ones more effectively while saving their own lives in the process. You make a choice each and every day to serve as a caregiver and I salute you with admiration and love.

# Contents

# What Others Are Saying

It is evident throughout the pages of this book that Michael Bloom has successfully integrated his own personal experience and story of caregiving for his parents with the powerful tools of iPEC's Core Energy Coach training to create this incredible resource for caregivers. He clearly identifies key challenges and offers up, with incredible clarity, tools and approaches that inspire solutions for caregivers struggling with the impact of what they do daily for those they love. I highly recommend this book to anyone on the path of caring for a loved one to be able generate a plan of self-care, self-compassion and support that will ensure their longevity as a caregiver so they can continue their mission of serving others in need.

Clearly, Michael Bloom has taken the lead in positively transforming the caregiver experience. Michael's work as a coach, motivational speaker and writer serves as a catalyst for energizing caregivers everywhere at a time when their service is so desired and needed.

**~ Tambre Leighn**

Michael - I am excited to see this in print...as you know this is a journey I have been on for a few years first with my father-in-law and now with my mother-in-law (who right now is as well as can be expected- except for her recent bout with shingles). My personal struggle is with feeling guilty that the burden of caregiving weighs me down- I know that's a normal feeling and this book has lightened the burden through validation of my feelings and solutions for addressing them.

You have done a wonderful job here of laying out in black and white the feelings and emotions brought about through the process of caregiving in a most supportive and beautiful way.

**~ Jean Phelps**

If you're feeling stifled—like you can't breathe under the heavy weight of medical crises, family conflict, or fear, you have made a wise choice to read this book.

Speaking with Michael Bloom is like taking a big gulp of fresh air. And fortunately, his written words have the same effect. So to read The Accidental Caregiver's Survival Guide: Your Roadmap to Caregiving Without Regret is to have your hand held while you are gently guided through the mire of stress, fear, and loss.

Actually, scratch that.

You're not being led by Michael Bloom's words—you're being empowered to lead yourself. That's the reality of caregiving. We aren't alone but we are mostly doing this by ourselves. We might be 65 million strong but we're still in crucial need of visibility and a voice. Hand-holding is sweet, but Bloom gives us legs to stand on.

If caregiving came about unexpectedly for you—or you feel like you're going in circles after years of caregiving—the message you'll find in The Accidental Caregiver's Survival Guide is clear, concise, and powerful.

We suggest you read one chapter a day—let go of that heavy weight one step at a time.

**~ Allie Axel**

# Chapter 1 – Introduction

Why do you need a roadmap to caregiving without regret?

> *"Two roads diverged in a wood, and I—*
> *I took the one less traveled by,*
> *And that has made all the difference."*
>
> ~ Robert Frost

Are you wondering, "How did I get here?"

The fact is, almost every single family caregiver throughout the world assumes his or her role accidentally and without pre-planning as a result of an unexpected family member illness, injury, or disability. When duty calls, the caregiver jumps right in to support the loved one in need without hesitation and puts other parts of their life on hold or on the back burner.

On August 23, 2009, my mother called me early in the morning with worry in her voice. I remember this call vividly as she told me that my father was acting "weird." Apparently, my father refused to prepare the morning medication at the start of their breakfast. As a retired chemist, he typically was very organized and regimented with each and every activity, so this was indeed strange. When my mother inquired about the medication, he frowned at her, angrily got off his chair, and stormed upstairs to his office and slammed the door. My mother, a five-year cancer survivor and frail 82-year-old, was afraid to follow him.

I drove over to their house right away. We lived only five miles apart and, as I drove, my mind raced with thoughts and possibilities as to what could be wrong. The previous afternoon during our daily phone chat, my father had shared some of the details of what he purchased at the grocery store. At that time, my father was a very healthy and independent 82-year-old. He was still driving and managing all household needs, including my mother's physical care, extremely well. During the call, he happily reported picking up an extra cantaloupe for me along with a few other food items that I could pick up at my convenience. Nothing seemed out of the ordinary during that conversation, so this anxious call from my mother was a bit shocking.

I arrived at my parents' house and briefly greeted my mother before going upstairs. I knocked on my father's office door and announced myself. A faint voice said "come in." When I opened the door, my father was sitting in his easy chair with his head drooping. I asked him how he was doing and he responded that he did not know. Fearing a stroke, I picked up the phone and called 911.

The EMTs arrived within 10 minutes. They discovered that my father had very low blood pressure and a heart rate of 25. He was taken to the emergency room and was treated for a catastrophic heart failure event. Later that day, a pacemaker was implanted and many additional tests followed. Unfortunately, my father lived the remainder of his life with vascular dementia as a result of the oxygen deprivation to his brain.

None of our lives would ever be the same. He instantly transformed into a person with severe memory loss and physical care needs that would require 24-hour support.

After five weeks of hospitalization, he returned home under my care and supervision. I never returned to fully live in my own home and ended up putting my house up for sale a year and half later. Instead, I fully dedicated myself as the full-time live-in supporter to both of my parents. As an only child who had a strong, deep, and precious relationship with both parents, I did not hesitate to jump right in and assume the role of family caregiver.

The journey of care is profound and transformational. Caregivers tend to be compassionate, dedicated, and selfless. Over time, they sacrifice sleep and self-care and may be just surviving with each passing week, month, or year on the brink of burnout.

Extremely busy days are the norm for caregivers with the feeling that they are swimming upstream to get all family tasks and needs met. Caregivers often, and understandably, put the needs of loved ones receiving care ahead of their own desires and goals. They pass on job opportunities, decrease work hours, or even leave jobs, which can diminish their own financial security. They may stop focusing on personal health and wellness by gaining or losing a significant amount of weight, which increases their own risk of serious illness or disease.

Caregivers usually devote little or no time to having fun with friends or intimate partners; thus, they become bored and depressed, with increasing isolation. They may give up personal hobbies and recreational activities that previously provided great fulfillment and joy.

Stress and worry dominate thoughts throughout each day, and the caregiver can even feel as though they are on the verge of collapse under the heavy burden of responsibilities. Basically, the life of a caregiver sadly transforms to one of all work, no play, and no joy.

If you are a family caregiver and experience some or all of the issues described above, you are not alone. So many people are experiencing increasing caregiving responsibilities and committing all of their time and effort to providing support to their loved ones. There are approximately 65 million caregivers in the United States alone who provide an annual estimated $450 billion value in services to their family members and friends, with these numbers expected to continue to grow rapidly with the aging population (The National Alliance for Caregiving, 2012).

There are many different types of family caregivers: people caring for life partners/spouses who become ill or disabled, parents caring for children with disabilities, adult children caring for aging parents, and family members caring for an injured veteran who returns from war, caring for a loved one who suffers a traumatic brain injury after a car or industrial accident, or caring for a loved one who is the victim of violence. Many caregivers even perform more than one caregiving role, such as providing care to an elderly parent with dementia and to a child with a disability—also referred to as a "sandwich generation" caregiver. Due to their dedication, limiting beliefs, and desire to do it all, many caregivers are highly stressed and on the brink of burnout. This puts their loved ones and themselves at risk of harm.

The good news is that with a renewed commitment to self it is possible to recharge your caregiving energy now and save your own life in the process. Think about it this way. Before an airplane takes off, the flight attendant shares emergency instructions. One of the primary directions is that when the oxygen masks drop overhead, it is vital for parents to place them on themselves before attending to their children. Otherwise, they run the risk of passing out, which could lead to death for both the parent and child. The same principle applies to effective caregiving. Apply the oxygen mask first to yourself, and then apply it to your loved one.

This book will pave your path to: confidently navigate through periods of crisis, overcome family conflict, achieve buy-in, lead your family and friends to contribute in meaningful ways, attract and retain the best expertise and talent, trust your intuition, create a rewarding life for yourself while serving as an inspiring caregiver, and transition to a new, meaningful life once the caregiving journey ends. Each section of the roadmap will be shared as a foundation principle that yields practical solutions to become a caregiver who lives free from regret.

The roadmap to caregiving without regret has been developed through much reflection and practical application of my personal caregiving journey as well as my work as a coach supporting fellow caregivers. It also incorporates aspects of research and theory, including Carl Jung's Personality Type Theory and Bruce Schneider's **Energy Leadership™ Paradigm.** Family caregivers are leaders—not just for their own lives, but also for the lives of their loved ones. It is so important for caregivers to manage and sustain their energy during the long journey of care.

Given the amazing contributions and dedication of caregivers, these leaders are also bright, shining lights in our world. As a caregiver, it is so important for you to take time for self-care so you can recharge your energy and keep your light shining brightly as a beacon of hope and support.

If you're feeling stifled—like you can't breathe under the heavy weight of medical crises, family conflict, or fear, you have made a wise choice to read this book.

It is time to apply your oxygen mask, take a deep breath, and take the journey to a life filled with more joy and satisfaction while providing high quality care you can be proud of. Then, after the caregiving journey comes to an end, you will be able to reflect and take comfort in a job well done and move forward free from regret.

# Chapter 2 – Release Crisis Mode

Stop being a victim of circumstances so you feel stronger and become laser-focused on meeting your family's needs.

*"Today is a new day. Don't let your history interfere with your destiny! Let today be the day you stop being a victim of your circumstances and start taking action towards the life you want. You have the power and the time to shape your life. Break free from the poisonous victim mentality and embrace the truth of your greatness. You were not meant for a mundane or mediocre life!"*

~ Steve Maraboli

The primary foundation principle on the road to caregiving without regret is to "release crisis mode." Given that the road traveled during the journey of care tends to be filled with potholes of medical and financial setbacks, it is so understandable that caregivers live in a state of crisis and fear. The caregiver walks hand-in-hand with the loved one through doctor's appointments, blood tests, medical scans, and associated therapies and treatment regimens. Although the patient is the one who directly experiences the physical and emotional pain through treatment, the caregiver cringes with every moan of their loved one and every troubling word of the doctor, leaving the caregiver feeling sad and helpless much of the time.

As the disappointments and painful moments accumulate while running back and forth to medical appointments, the pharmacy, and other care-related errands, the caregiver can become consumed with fear and believe they are living under a dark cloud of doom and gloom. Although many caregivers perform heroically and show a positive face to support their loved ones, they can break down physically and emotionally over time if they dwell too much on what they cannot control.

Why does this happen? Caregivers often lead solitary lives that can leave them feeling all alone and isolated. When they choose to embark on the journey alone and without support, anger, anxiety, depression, sadness, and worry can linger for days or weeks at a time.

It is also important to point out that caregivers are susceptible to the stages of grief throughout the caregiving journey. Grief can be defined as deep mental anguish that typically arises after the death of a loved one. The Kübler-Ross model, commonly referred to as the "five stages of grief," is a hypothesis introduced by Elisabeth Kübler-Ross. She asserts that when a person, whether a survivor, caregiver, or loved one, is faced with the reality of impending death or some other extreme, awful fate, he or she will experience a series of emotional "stages": denial; anger; bargaining; depression; and, finally, acceptance. These stages will emerge during the caregiving journey in no specific sequence, meaning one stage does not follow another in a linear progression.

It is important to recognize that any of the grief stages can come to the forefront for the caregiver or loved one during many points along the journey of care, and sometimes they arise more than once. The feelings of sadness and despair can be overwhelming and it is important for caregivers to seek support, especially when they feel paralyzed in a stage of grief.

Otherwise, in an effort to control the feelings of fear and hopelessness, the caregiver can be susceptible to turning to alcohol, drugs, or overeating. For some caregivers, raiding the refrigerator and food cabinets at night for high-calorie snacks or downing a sedative with a stiff drink might lead to a temporary numbing and relief from the overwhelming fear and sadness. Caregivers who turn to this type of self-defeating treatment may only make matters worse.

Let me clarify that I do not have an issue with prescription medications if they are prescribed under the close supervision of a physician. After all, a caregiver who is struggling to sleep may benefit from a sleep aid to get quality overnight rest.

It is vital that family caregivers not ignore their own health and regularly see their doctors for consultation and treatment. Unfortunately, family caregivers tend to see their own health care providers less during the heavy demands of the caregiving journey since they can grow weary of attending all the medical appointments with their loved ones.

Instead of waiting for an emergency or illness to schedule a visit with a primary care physician, a family caregiver would be better served to increase routine and preventative doctor visits to three or four times per year. Partnering with your primary care physician to regularly discuss your caregiving stress may serve to keep you free of an undesired illness or hospitalization.

The path to successfully releasing crisis mode and the racing thoughts associated with anxiety and worry about the
care for your loved one begins with acceptance. As a family
caregiver, you deserve much admiration for making the courageous choice each and every day to serve as a caregiver.

You may be asking, "What choice? I don't have a choice.
I have to take care of my parent/my partner/my child." The
truth is everyone has a choice. Every caregiver could truly
walk away at any time. Some of us are fortunate to have
beautiful, positive, and inspiring people to support. For others, the loved one may be grumpy, stubborn, and challenging
to support. When the caregiver wakes up in the morning and
begins the tasks associated with care, a choice is being made
to serve and do those things. Start to give yourself credit for
making this choice and feel the positivity of the power in
that choice as you accept your role as a dedicated caregiver
for another day.

This may not be easy. For example, I connected with a
family caregiver named Marge (her name was named changed
to preserve confidentiality) who reported taking care of her
elderly father for several years and found herself resenting
him more and more with each passing day. She was adopted
as a young child and never felt appreciated or wanted by her
father. She did not know if this was because her father would
have preferred to have a son or not to have a child at all.

Marge's mother was the natural caregiver in the family.
Marge shared that her mother showed her and her father
unconditional love and support throughout her life.

Her father, on the other hand, was always very negative
and complained about all aspects of his life, including his
responsibilities for his daughter. Marge reported never feeling

any acceptance or love from her father, so she spent much of the time avoiding his company. After the death of her mother, her father was living alone and in ill health. Given her inspiring dedication to her mother and her religious faith, Marge felt compelled to step in and provide primary, live-in caregiving support to her father.

Unfortunately, when Marge contacted me she described feeling at wits' end and in a perpetual state of emotional crisis. Throughout each day, she did not know when to expect another onslaught of anger and name-calling from her father. I could feel her pain when describing her day-to-day life and state of mind.

It was understandable why she was feeling so depressed and burned out with this caregiving situation. She had given up everything, including her career and home, to support her father. She was feeling guilty for having feelings of resentment toward her father and hoped that by staying and supporting him that she would please God. She was feeling hopeless, powerless, and trapped in her situation but held onto a strong belief of faith that her reward would come in the next life. In the meantime, she was losing more of herself with each passing day and felt little hope for ever enjoying another day in this life.

There are several options for caregivers to consider when dealing with a loved one like Marge's father. To release crisis mode and the perpetual feeling of being a victim, caregivers will empower themselves through acceptance and the belief that they are making a conscious choice to serve as a caregiver for another day. This acceptance also applies to being at peace with who the loved one receiving care is as a person.

Although one may powerfully choose to accept who their

loved one is, that does not mean that the caregiver needs to accept harmful or painful treatment such as physical or verbal abuse. How can this situation be navigated? Let's explore some of the options.

**Option 1:** Do nothing. Just keep doing what you are doing and hope for a different result. Of course, you run the risk of becoming caregiver toast and completely losing yourself in the process. One popular definition of insanity is doing the same thing again and again and expecting a different result. It is not recommended to fall into this vicious cycle or you run the risk of spending most of each day feeling like a victim.

**Option 2:** Leave the situation. Marge can tell her father that she is no longer going to serve as his caregiver due to his abusive treatment of her. He will likely end up in a nursing home and she can try to piece her independent life back together. She will probably live each day filled with guilt and with a feeling of betraying her religious beliefs. Although this can be a heart-wrenching decision, not everyone is capable of serving as a primary, live-in caregiver for a loved one for the long term. Even when you do not believe there is a choice, if you feel mistreated, isolated, and trapped, seek some immediate professional support. Your physician, a therapist, or a social worker can serve as good resources to help you navigate successfully through your difficult situation. If you are on the verge of collapse or the feeling that you need to walk away, do not delay. Set aside some time to research options and determine what care services may be better in the long run for you and your loved one.

**Option 3:** Use acceptance and set clear expectations. The foundation for this option is for Marge to accept her father for who he is and herself for being a dedicated, yet imperfect caregiver. It is important to point out that accepting her father for who he is does not mean that she needs to accept any verbally or physically abusive behavior. It is vital that Marge set clear expectations so that her father understands what is necessary if he wants to continue to receive Marge's caregiving support so he can "age in place" in his home.

Before engaging in this understandably challenging discussion, Marge would benefit from making a list of all the things to share with her father that would make life better for her so she can serve as his caregiver for the long term. One way to do this in an organized fashion is to write a draft expectation agreement to be shared. Written agreements can bring clarity to expectations and help people consistently and satisfactorily meet those expectations. Here is a sample of a caregiving expectation description.

As your caregiver, I will strive to:

- Provide you with the best possible care.

- Respect you and the choices you make.

- Share my opinions in a calm and supportive manner—even when we do not agree.

- Seek specialized supports when your care needs require them to keep you safe.

- Complete activities of self-care that will give me the ability to take better care of you over the long term.

- Be open to receiving support from others with specific tasks and responsibilities.

- Maintain parts of my own life while I care for you so I develop a satisfying life for myself beyond caregiving.

- Admit when I make a mistake or have moments when emotions lead me to do or say something I later regret.

- Give and receive acceptance, affection, consideration, and forgiveness during our journey of care.

As your loved one receiving care, I will strive to:

- Openly communicate my concerns, fears, and needs.

- Respect you and the choices you make.

- Share my opinions in a calm and supportive manner—even when we do not agree.

- Be willing to receive specialized supports from others when my care needs require them to keep me safe.

- Support your desire to maintain parts of your own life while you care for me.

- Be open to receiving support from others with specific tasks and responsibilities.

- Follow treatment plans and protocols from my medical support team.

- Try my best to not use anger or guilt to get you to do things for me.

- Admit when I make a mistake or have moments when emotions lead me to do or say something I later regret.

- Give and receive acceptance, affection, consideration, and forgiveness during our journey of care.

Feel free to add to or revise parts of this agreement to reflect language that you and your loved one are comfortable with. It is also strongly suggested that you get input from your loved one for additions and revisions before finalizing. Use of an agreement like this can serve as a successful vehicle for a thorough and satisfying discussion of needs for both you and your loved one. Note that you can access a copy of this agreement as a bonus by registering free of charge for "Your Caregiving Burnout Risk Assessment" at www.BurnoutRisk.com.

Once this agreement is in effect for a period of time, it can be useful to sit down and review how well you both are doing. You both can take time to rate on a scale of 1-10 how well you are doing with each of the agreed-upon components. When engaging in such a review, focus first on what is working well and reinforce your loved one for taking this seriously. Use the focused discussion as an opportunity to shower your loved one with appreciation for progress.

Next, you can target the lowest-rated items and set goals to address them together. The idea is to partner with your loved one so he or she feels empowered to safely express opinions and play an important role in the goal-setting exercise.

For some caregivers, especially those serving loved ones who are suffering with Alzheimer's disease, dementia, or other cognitive disabilities, this option may not work as easily. Empower your loved one with as much choice and input as they can provide. The core of the power of this agreement for the caregiver is actually in their self-ratings for how they are handling their own expectations. After all, the higher the ratings on the caregiver part of the agreement, the more likely the caregiver is to accept their role, avoid burnout, and release crisis mode.

Remember, acceptance is the key to peace, joy, and satisfaction throughout your life.

When we accept important people in our lives for who they are, we can communicate, partner, and support them with greater ease.

When we accept things that happen that are beyond our control, we can move beyond them more quickly, free from blame and feeling overwhelmed.

When we accept ourselves for where we are now, we can release fear, guilt, and the belief that we are not good enough; this allows us to keep moving forward with intention and purpose.

Here is one additional suggested practice tip for when those out-of-control situations emerge. When feeling a moment of fear or a state of crisis, take a deep breath and say the serenity prayer out loud (from "The Serenity Prayer," attributed to Reinhold Niebuhr).

*Grant me the serenity*
*To accept the things I cannot change,*
*Courage to change the things I can,*
*and wisdom to know the difference.*

After any time you choose to say the serenity prayer, focus and identify one small action you can take that will move you forward and please you. Once you identify this acceptance-inspired action, either complete it immediately or schedule time in your calendar or day planner to do it.

Choose not to live in reaction mode to your life or circumstances or you will just barely survive each day feeling like a victim. No matter how prepared you are and how agreeable your loved one is, it is natural to still have some days and times when you feel extremely down and worried. The important thing is not to stay there day after day. Take one small, imperfect, and inspired action to feel more in control of your life and more capable of dealing with any situation you face. Believe in the power of your resiliency and determination.

# Chapter 3 –
# Overtake Conflict

Communicate calmly and clearly with your loved one and other family members as you ride the emotional roller coasters associated with the disability or disease and cope with any situation—no matter what.

*"The most intense conflicts, if overcome, leave behind a sense of security and calm that is not easily disturbed. It is just these intense conflicts and their conflagration which are needed to produce valuable and lasting results."*

~ Carl Jung

The second foundation principle on the road to caregiving without regret is to "overtake conflict." The journey of care is not easy, as it can feel like riding emotional roller coasters filled with challenging loops of heart-wrenching decisions. Given the depth and seriousness of the choices, it is not surprising that differences of opinions may emerge among all of the involved parties.

The primary caregiver usually takes the lead in facilitating and supporting treatment decisions for the loved one. It is important to keep in mind that a loved one who is an adult and free from dementia is capable of making his or her own decisions. After all, we all want to feel as independent

19

as possible throughout our lives. We spend our childhoods yearning to achieve full independence, and we will struggle during our weakest times toward the end of life to hold onto it.

Each of us deserves the right to make our choices and decisions when it comes to our bodies. And, to be fully alive and growing, we each deserve the right to take risks.

Even those who have dementia or disabilities deserve to be given as many opportunities to make choices as possible. Choice is the key to feeling fully alive. Many of us take for granted the large number of choices we make throughout our day such as: what time to get up and start the day, what clothes to wear, what foods to eat, what songs to listen to, what television shows to watch, what websites to surf, and what time to go to bed.

One of the ways to demonstrate care and respect is to provide as many opportunities as possible for choice to loved ones receiving care. Unfortunately, conflict with our loved ones over choices and decisions can serve as one of main challenges during the caregiving journey.

For example, I can recall a coaching session with an adult daughter who was helping to care for her 63-year-old father during his battle with cancer; she reported an argument over his eating habits. The daughter chose to live a healthy life-style filled with exercise and the consumption of raw fruits and vegetables. She was extremely knowledgeable about the nutritional value of certain foods and had literature to support the potential benefits of those foods in strengthening the immune system, especially during cancer treatment.

She would instruct (aka, lecture) her father about what he was eating and, to her dismay, her father did not share these values. Her brother would bring in high-calorie, high-fat snacks and treats, which the father enjoyed and readily ate. Meanwhile, her containers of healthy food and drinks would sit untouched. During one visit, all three of them started arguing over the food choices and had a miserable visit together.

During one of our coaching sessions, I asked the daughter to try to take her father's perspective and consider why he might be making the eating choices. She informed me that the oncologist had shared at the last appointment that the cancer was no longer responding favorably to treatment and that the prognosis was not looking good. Her father was also considering stopping treatment, and this was very upsetting because she felt as though he was just giving up.

She was able to articulate with logic that her father probably believed he had limited time left. Since he did not expect to be able to eat much of anything for much longer, he wanted to experience the taste of food that he would enjoy. We also processed that her brother was not bringing in the high-calorie snacks to kill their father. An alternate interpretation was that he was bringing in those foods to show his appreciation and love for their father with things that could be enjoyed.

After reviewing the alternate interpretations for the actions of her brother and father, we were able to process a new approach for her next visit. During that visit something amazing happened.

Although she still brought in her portable cooler of healthy snacks and drinks, she did not pull anything out of it to show her father. Instead, they had a calm, clear, and warm conversation. She acknowledged that he might have limited time left and that she understood that he wanted to enjoy it as much as possible.

She told him that she would no longer lecture him on what types of food to eat and would respect his choices. She also committed to no longer yell at her brother for bringing in his snacks since she knew he only did it out of love.

She admitted feeling powerless to help her father and that his disease was frightening. Bringing healthy foods served as a way to give herself some comfort and feel as though she was helping. She told her father that she loved him and that those special foods would be available to him should he choose to try any of them. If not, she would just take them home and enjoy them herself.

The two of them went on that day to have a pleasant conversation. Later during the visit, her father asked to look into her cooler. He opened it up and took a few bites of the healthy foods she brought, followed by a chocolate chip cookie chaser (one of the items dropped off the previous day by his son).

After that day, there was no more conflict over nutritional and treatment decisions. The father did decide to stop cancer treatment and sadly passed away about four weeks later under the caring support of his daughter, son, and a hospice team. He did it his way and enjoyed his special treats until his last few days here on earth.

The key to overcoming conflict is to communicate calmly, clearly, and openly. Avoid lecturing and the use of "should statements," as they put the other person on the defensive.

It is much more effective to provide advice and information to others, acknowledge their circumstances and your respect for their choices, and let them make the decisions. Try not to take it personally if the other person does not make the choices you believe to be right. Sometimes, if you let it settle without argument or pressure, you may be pleasantly surprised to see the other integrate some of what you share.

So what happens when someone lectures or uses "should statements" with you? As the primary caregiver for my parents, I found this happening a lot.

During the three years I lived with my parents, I heard statements like, "You should consider putting your mother in a nursing home. You are still young and need to live your own life." Whenever I heard statements like this, the hair would stand up on the back of my neck and I would get very tense and clench my fists. It is natural to feel defensive during these situations. The way to avoid conflict is to take a deep breath and acknowledge (but not validate) the statement.

For example, my response to the statement above became, "I appreciate your concern for me and my quality of life. Thank you. For now, I am committed to caring for my mom and taking one day at a time." This strategy was always successful and usually got a quick response such as "OK, keep thinking about it and be good to yourself." There would not be an argument, and it was easy to transition peacefully to another topic.

Conflict can be avoided or resolved quickly when you communicate your beliefs and needs calmly and without judgment. Friends and family members share information out of care and love. Unfortunately, information is not always presented in an attractive and convincing way.

Even if you do not follow what is shared, respect yourself and the opinions of others to open yourself up to learning new information and possibilities to solve the issues of the day. This can lead to useful collaboration and a much more energetic and positive caregiving journey.

It is so easy to fall into conflict mode. We are surrounded by it—on reality television, in social media posts, in workplace interactions, and in many other situations. Conflict tends to be a successful strategy for people to get what they want. Unfortunately, this strategy takes an "I win and you lose" or "I am right and you are wrong" approach. Although this approach can be effective in getting what you want in the short term, it can be very physically and emotionally draining over time for you and your family. What if there were a different, less costly and draining approach to take? After all, caregiving is not a political campaign, so try not to follow the lead of our politicians, especially as seen during debates and in political advertisements. Politicians raise lots of money to promote messages that tend to be misleading, negative, and for the purpose of bashing an opponent.

If you can successfully master the ability to navigate and overtake conflict, your world will become more peaceful and satisfying. Once you commit to finding a "we all benefit" approach, it will be much easier to achieve buy-in from even those you tend to disagree with much of the time. This will be a focus of the next chapter.

In the meantime, try to communicate all ideas, messages, and needs calmly and clearly. When you receive input from others that you do not agree with, express appreciation for the feedback and let them know that it will be considered. After all, what initially sounds unworkable or troubling may actually be useful if you give yourself more time to ponder it.

At a time when you and your family are in need of love and support, you do not want to take an attitude of anger that can push people away and leave you feeling more isolated. Express an attitude of gratitude as well as openness to a diversity of opinion. This will help you build a better care-giving support team as you ride the emotional roller coasters associated with the disability or disease so you can cope with any situation—no matter what.

# Chapter 4 –
# Achieve Buy-In

Motivate others to contribute based upon their individual abilities, preferences, and talents so your loved one receives the most satisfying support possible.

*"Leadership is the art of getting someone else to do something you want done because he wants to do it."*

~ Dwight D. Eisenhower

The third foundation principle on the road to caregiving without regret is to "achieve buy-in." The person stricken with an illness, disease, or disability typically has a lot of involved parties—family members, friends, doctors, nurses, social workers, and other specialists.

Everyone involved is usually filled with opinions concerning abilities, prognosis, and support needs. Conflict, as described in the previous chapter, can creep in and take over when calm, clear, and open communication is not used.

One of the most empowering and important roles that the primary caregiver can assume is leader. The most effective caregiver leaders are great listeners and astute observers. They listen carefully to what others say by acknowledging and validating various opinions and points of view. They observe the actions, skills, and talents of others and find ways to make use of them.

The main complaint that primary caregivers tend to have is that others are not stepping up to the plate and doing what should be done to support the loved one in need. Caregivers who hold tightly to this judgmental mindset tend to ask for support ineffectively. They can be perceived as demanding, judging, and dictatorial to others, which may result in a few things getting done but rarely leads to ongoing and committed support.

Caregivers who lead through coercion and demands actually put their own roadblocks on the journey to effective caregiving. People do not like being told what they should do. Adult siblings or other family members also may avoid helping when called to complete one particular task. This tends to happen because the person being asked feels pressured to complete an undesirable or challenging task.

Other family members and friends are more likely to say yes to requests for support if they are provided with choices. All of us enjoy having choices and there are certainly a whole bunch of activities and tasks that can be done to support the caregiver or loved one receiving support. If you are having difficulty securing help from other family members, try giving them a menu of helpful tasks to select from and see what happens.

In reality, many key family members and friends may wish deep down that they could help. Some people who are most willing to help the caregiver may not know exactly how. When they ask in general "How can I help?" the caregiver may respond by saying that it is under control or that he or she cannot think of anything that they can do.

It is normal to not want to burden others with our issues or responsibilities. Meanwhile, we have supporters who are so willing to share their skills and talents with us if they are just given the chance and the choice of specific ways they can be of assistance.

The path to efficient and high-quality care is to create attractive ways for others to maximize individual abilities, talents, and preferences. This is done by creating a caregiving support plan. Again, one of the biggest challenges for some caregivers, especially those who may be considered control freaks, is the belief that it would take longer to train someone else how to do something than to do it themselves. While this may be certain for some caregiving tasks, it is not true for all.

The first step to developing an effective caregiving support plan is to list all the tasks that you complete as a caregiver. Typically, responsibilities fall into three main categories: household, medical, and social supports. All three categories have many parts. A fourth category (miscellaneous) is also useful to include in your planning in order to list family-specific tasks that may fall outside of the three major categories.

Household supports can include: cleaning, laundry, meal and menu planning, food shopping, meal preparation, supply shopping, banking, and minor household maintenance and repair.

Medical supports can include: transportation to physician/dental/therapy/lab testing appointments, transportation to dialysis or other medical treatments, medication pick-up and administration, tracking of vitals (blood pressure, pulse, weight, blood sugar monitoring, and oxygen level), and physical support with bathing and topical treatments.

Social supports can include: transportation and company

for social groups and restaurant trips, companionship for playing games or watching movies/sports, hobbies such as knitting or painting, and providing supervision so the primary caregiver can have respite time for other activities.

Once you have identified the initial activities and items of your caregiving support plan, the next step is to make a list of all the family members and friends that you have in your life who may be of support. List everyone even if you think they may not be available, skilled, or willing to help. Think outside of your box of biases, as you may be surprised to learn who may willingly step up to the plate to help with certain preferred tasks.

Once you have brainstormed all potential supporters, take one person at a time and make a list of their hobbies, skills, and talents. For some people, you may only think of one, and for others you may think of a bunch. For this exercise, include the children and teenagers in your life. You might be surprised to learn that they can also be of useful social support to your loved one.

For example, a teenage grandson who enjoys talking on the phone, watching sports, and playing games could be a good person to visit their elderly grandfather (who is the father you are caring for). He might be asked if he would be interested in participating in a call rotation with other family members so grandpa can talk to at least one person that he loves every day. He might visit two or three times per month to watch a baseball game on television while completing a jigsaw puzzle with grandpa.

During these pre-planned and -scheduled visits, you, the primary caregiver, can run errands or do a fun recreational or leisure activity while grandfather and grandson happily spend quality time together. More importantly, a young family member learns that she or he is valued and can make important contributions to the family.

Once you have a list of family and friends with their hobbies, skills, and talents, look back at your task list from your draft caregiving support plan. For the different tasks that you have listed, you can start to identify people who may be able to complete them on a periodic or routine basis. Start approaching people and sharing your task list and see what people show an interest in doing.

The best way to achieve buy-in is to let people choose and self-select what they can do to contribute. Once activities are completed, reinforce them and watch the positive energy become contagious, thereby encouraging others to do more and getting other family members involved.

What if involving others in support does not seem like a viable option? This is another question and frequent complaint from many primary caregivers due to the limiting belief that their loved one will only do things with them.

One former coaching client (whom I will call Jill) lived with this limiting belief for a period of several intensive months. Her mother was becoming increasingly fragile and in need of more frequent support. The problem was that mother and daughter lived 200 miles apart.

Jill had taken a number of days off from work to attend medical appointments and run errands such as food shopping for her mother. She was spending every weekend at the mother's home. This was becoming unsustainable as she grew worried about the effect on her ability to perform her job and the absence from her family back home.

During one conversation, Jill expressed frustration that

her mother and brother had had a falling out ten years earlier and did not speak. The brother lived in the same town
as the mother and could have been of great support. The
client expressed a wish to me that the brother would come
in and help but felt hopeless that the differences could ever
be resolved.

She reported also finding her mother to be difficult to
deal with at times, but they had never had a falling out due
to her own patience and silence. She and her brother did
have a positive relationship. After fully processing the family
dynamics and her internal blocks, a plan to achieve buy-in
was developed.

First, Jill planned to have separate conversations with her
mother and brother. During these conversations, she would
share concerns about the amount of time she was devoting to
meeting all of her mother's needs and the negative impact it
was having on her life. She would explain that she was committed to continuing to help her mother but needed assistance
so she did not burn out or become ill herself. By making these
conversations open and honest about her own needs, both her
mother and brother expressed a willingness (to her amaze-
ment) to get together to talk. The following weekend they all
met at the mother's house and shared a pizza.

The visit went much better than expected as Jill developed
a script and took the lead in the conversation. She expressed
her wish that her mother and brother could get along so they
could plan and work together to meet their mother's needs
so she could successfully stay in her home.

By placing the focus of the conversation on Jill's concern
and how the others could support Jill so everyone could be
successful, buy-in was achieved. When talking about things

in the house that were in need of some repair, the brother's eyes lit up, as he shared some of the repairs that he would be happy to do.

The following Tuesday after work, the brother came over for dinner and did a little repair work in the house. This got the ball rolling, and soon he became an active participant in supporting the mother.

Jill was then able to decrease the frequency of her visits and the foundation was set for a collaborative and more satisfying caregiving journey. The bottom line: release some limiting beliefs that family dynamics are permanent. Everything in life is fluid, and buy-in can be achieved if all possibilities remain open.

By mastering the foundation principle of "achieving buy-in," you will more easily utilize others in ways that maximize their individual abilities, preferences, and talents so your loved one receives the highest-quality and most satisfying supports possible. This will also provide freedom for living your own life more fully.

# Chapter 5 –
# Deliver Greatness

Become the inspiring caregiver that people cheer for and gladly support in meaningful ways.

*"Not everybody can be famous but everybody can be great, because greatness is determined by service."*

~ Martin Luther King, Jr.

The fourth foundation principle on the road to caregiving without regret is to "deliver greatness" so you can become the inspiring caregiver that people cheer for and gladly support in meaningful ways. The roadblock that most often prevents us from delivering greatness is the persistent draining of our stress-busting reservoirs. This can lead to exhaustion, illness, and a nasty attitude.

The path to delivering greatness as a caregiver is forged through self-care. People who commit to taking care of themselves first (remember the oxygen mask example from Chapter 1) will sustain the power and ability to provide compassionate, quality care to their loved ones for the long term. In this chapter, we are going to focus on the sources of self-care that will fuel the success and sustainability of the inspirational caregiver.

One of the main ways to fuel your caregiving energy is

to take time to enjoy consistent and nutritious meals. Meals are often something we rush through. We may pick up a coffee and a quick breakfast at a drive-through and consume it as we drive to work or go about our morning activities. We may work through lunch, skip lunch, or eat a few bites while working at our desk. Sitting down to dinner with the family may be something that we do once or twice per week if we are lucky. As we are more connected through technological gadgets, we are not only sacrificing work/life balance but are actually losing a fundamental activity that fuels our life... mealtime.

If we take the time to actually enjoy a good meal, we can give ourselves the necessary recharge to become more productive between meals. When was the last time you took a full hour to enjoy one meal? Or even a half hour? If you cannot remember and you are feeling increasing amounts of stress, this practice tip is for you.

Practice Tip: Sit down for your next meal, preferably with other people, and just enjoy leisurely conversation or listen to music (if alone) as you dine. If you really want to take the meal to a great place of peace and relaxation, light some candles. Dining by candlelight is such a relaxing treat that generations have enjoyed for centuries. It is time for more of us to return to fully nourishing our stomachs and souls at mealtimes.

The second aspect of quality self-care is to get enough quality sleep. Unfortunately, caregivers often start the day tired after a night of difficult and interrupted sleep.

One of the primary culprits of sleep deprivation is our unsettled minds. At night, it can be challenging to fall asleep at a decent time because we have disturbing and stressful thoughts running through our heads. These thoughts may include: things we have done that we wish we had done better, a recent troubling appointment or interaction, worry about financial and medical issues, or anticipation of challenging tasks and responsibilities over the coming days with co-workers or family members.

On many days, it may seem difficult to find the time to complete the most routine tasks for ourselves. We do manage to take care of regular hygiene tasks such as tooth brushing. Why? We know that taking a few minutes each day to complete this physical task that we were trained to do as children will help us avoid cavities and uncomfortable trips to the dentist. We also take care of the inanimate objects we value, such as automobiles. We take our vehicles for routine maintenance, and if a "check engine" light goes on, we make an appointment to see the mechanic right away.

Unfortunately, most of us have not been trained to take care of our own stress, so we don't regularly set aside time to deal with our stress. We were also not created with a "check stress level" light in our heads to alert us to deal with it now. The good news, however, is that we can set brief, regular appointments with ourselves to get those stressful thoughts out of our heads.

**Practice Tip:** Schedule a 10-minute time block in your schedule at least once per week to relieve your mind of stressful thoughts. During your scheduled time, think of everything in your life that is concerning you in that moment and write it down. Once you have finished making your list, read it and star the item that stresses you out the most. Read the item closely and notice how you feel. Do not judge your-self. Instead, breathe deeply and give yourself per-mission to feel what you are feeling. Just provide love and understanding to yourself as you would to a good friend.

On nights that you are having trouble falling asleep because you have a mind racing with thoughts, you can do this exercise. Keep a notepad on your nightstand. The act of taking the items physically out of your head and putting them on paper should help to settle your mind so you can get that needed sleep.

If you schedule the 10-minute weekly worry session with yourself to complete this exercise, you may find over time that sleep will come much more easily to you, and you can feel more energized each day. By designating times that deal-ing with stress and worry are not just okay, but encouraged, you will be taking proactive steps to reduce your level of burnout and that dreaded nasty attitude.

It is worth repeating that regularly engaging (at least once per week) in this stress cleansing exercise can work won-ders to stop those sleep-busting thoughts from rolling around your head all night and leaving you as a grumpy and overtired caregiver during the day. In order to keep those thoughts from resurfacing again and again, it is beneficial to review your stress list and generate a list of tasks from the list.

Once you have a list of tasks, you can then make plans to complete them and seek assistance from others who are skilled or talented in certain areas. Add these tasks to your caregiving support plan as described in Chapter 4.

Caregivers can also benefit from having fun and engaging

in soul-soothing activities. Many caregivers avoid this due to perceived financial and time limitations. However, there are very simple and fun activities that can be done along with your routine and that cost nothing.

One such easy and free activity is listening to motivational music to help you relax and be more productive. Do you remember driving or riding in a car as a young person or teenager blasting your favorite song on your radio or music player? I can recall driving home from high school in my teenage years after a long, sometimes stressful school day and recharging myself by singing away my blues (sometimes with the window open, to the dismay or entertainment of neighboring drivers). Once I returned home and completed the last song, I was usually ready to tackle homework or the daily chores.

Just because we are grown up with major caregiving and leadership responsibilities does not mean that the simple things like listening to our favorite songs can't give us a much-needed fun break and get us back into motivated action.

**Practice Tip:** Think of your favorite song and find it on your iPod or in your CD collection (or even your cassette/vinyl collection). Or you can even just go to YouTube now and see if you find a video with your song. Play it, get off your chair, and sing/dance/ move with the music. Any time you need a quick energy burst and recharge, try this simple practice. Music does work wonders for the soul!

One of the most significant ways to deliver greatness as

you aspire to become an inspirational caregiver whom others gladly support can also be the most difficult—acknowledging that you are human and make mistakes. Nobody is perfect.

Even those of us who are extremely conscientious can make an error. Sometimes, when overtired, a caregiver may forget an appointment, misplace mail or keys, or make a late bill payment. Caregiver mistakes may lead to frustration, self-criticism, and grumpiness. When in this state, the caregiver may be susceptible to a short fuse and lash out in a burst of anger.

*"Anger is the most impotent of passions. It effects nothing it goes about, and hurts the one who is possessed by it more than the one against whom it is directed."*

~ Carl Sandburg

It is during these times of stress that the caregiver may even yell or say something regretful to the loved one receiving care. In fact, one of the biggest sources of hurt and disappointment I have heard is the regret that the caregiver had for things said during periods of stress. Again, nobody is perfect. Loved ones have tremendous understanding for the stress you may be under.

Don't let regret build up over unresolved anger outbursts. More importantly, don't let yourself fall into a common caregiver trap of unrelenting guilt over your perceptions and biased interpretations of how you treated your loved one. This can bring great turmoil to a caregiver and impede healing during the journey of grief after the loved one's passing.

Anger is one of the key stages of grief. Grief can be experienced at many points during the caregiving journey, not just after someone dies. Don't knock yourself for the times that you feel angry. Forgive yourself and apologize to anyone you may lash out at. By acknowledging your humanness and expressing remorse for any hurt you may have brought to another, you can more readily return to the journey of caregiving without regret.

On a personal note, I can recall several days when I became a little sharp-tongued with my mother when my stress levels were running high and I felt nagged about completing certain tasks a certain way. No matter how much we love the person we are caring for, sometimes things can get under our skin.

Fortunately, these anger events or disagreements were few and far between. A rule I set for myself was never to go to bed angry or leave a previous disagreement unresolved. By following this rule of acknowledging my stress and apologizing for any hurt I may have caused, my mother easily shared her forgiveness. On a few occasions, she did not even understand why I was apologizing since she did not even feel hurt or slighted.

As the Sandburg quotation states, anger can hurt the one who is possessed by it more than the one against whom it was directed. Whether it affects your loved one or not, openly share your feelings and sorrow so you can more easily move forward with peace of mind. Forgive yourself for expressing this common human emotion. Then set the intention to move forward and deliver greatness as an inspiring yet imperfect caregiver.

**Practice Tip:** When your stress balloon has burst and you get angry, let it out. Acknowledge yourself for having a truly human feeling. Take some space and process what may be contributing to this anger.

You may want to follow the practice tip shared earlier in this chapter regarding how to cleanse your mind of stressful thoughts. Once you have calmed down and regained your sense of composure, seek out the person who witnessed or bore the brunt of your outburst and make peace with a genuine and heartfelt apology. This will give you the resolve to put that event in the past and move forward into another courageous caregiving day.

Important Note: Anger that grips you such that you feel at risk of harming yourself or another person needs immediate attention. It is vital that you never take your anger out physically on another. If you believe yourself to be on the verge of expressing anger in a potentially harmful way, seek professional support from your physician or a therapist as soon as possible.

The final and most important way to deliver greatness and inspire others to provide you and your loved one with support is through gratitude. Taking time to reflect and share gratitude can work wonders for the soul of a caregiver. Even if you are spending lots of time under stress and not ready to commit to living a full life of gratitude, giving yourself and others brief moments of gratitude can be positively infectious.

**Practice Tip:** Brainstorm a list of things that friends, family members, and co-workers have done over the past year that you are grateful for. Once you have this list, make a phone call or share your specific item of gratitude face-to-face with the person(s).

You can begin the conversation with the statement, "I am grateful for..." If you want to reflect with gratitude for a loved one who has passed away, write it down and share out loud. Filling your heart with gratitude for things that have occurred, are currently happening, or that you are setting the intention to happen in the future can be so energizing. Adopt an attitude of gratitude and you will find that others will be inspired to have your back and support you in service to your loved one.

Caregivers can more readily deliver greatness when their physical, emotional, and spiritual needs are being met. By focusing on being compassionate to yourself, you will demonstrate much more compassion to others. Don't fall into a caregiver trap of believing that self-care is selfish. It definitely isn't!

Caregivers who focus on self-care with nutrition, sleep, stress reduction, and gratitude will equip and fuel themselves for serving their loved ones with dedication and inspiration for the long term. Continue to learn, share, and grow with family, friends, and specialized professionals. This will help you to escape the island of caregiver isolation and create your own satisfying life.

# Chapter 6 –
# Magnetize and
# Motivate Talent

C reate an atmosphere that attracts and retains the best people to join your loved one's care team, and experience brilliant performance.

*"Human resources are like natural resources;*
*they're often buried deep. You have to go looking for them;*
*they're not just lying around on the surface.*
*You have to create the circumstances where they show themselves."*
~ Ken Robinson

The fifth foundation principle on the road to caregiving without regret is to "magnetize and motivate talent." When you have mastered the principle to "deliver greatness" with the adoption of the attitude of gratitude, talented supporters will be magnetized and motivated to share their talent.

My mother exemplified this principle throughout her life. She exuded caring, gratitude, and respect to everyone who had the privilege of crossing her path. Total strangers were always moved to share the most personal of details as they soaked in her warm smile.

I am grateful that I had eight additional years with her, as she was not expected to survive her original fight with cancer in 2004. At that time, she was diagnosed with Stage 4B Hodgkin's disease as a 77-year-old woman. My mother had a very high threshold for pain, so we did not become aware of her disease until she unexpectedly passed out in a store one day and was taken to the emergency room for testing and evaluation.

She was assigned to a skilled oncologist who was concerned about her ability to tolerate the chemotherapy. The oncologist was confident that the proposed chemotherapy had great potential for cure but pointed out that my mother's state of frailty put her at risk of having the chemo kill her before the cancer.

After hearing this news, my mother looked at the worried faces of my father and me. She then turned to the oncologist and said with a smile, "You are going to cure me. Let's do it!"

Sure enough, six months later with a set of clean scans, the oncologist referred to my mother as her little miracle. My parents and I left the medical appointment that day with beaming smiles and a celebratory lunch.

Although my mother survived the treatment, the chemotherapy did forever leave her frail and with challenging neuropathy and balance issues. She would require significant physical support and numerous medical appointments for the remainder of her life. At times, she got a bit down about her limitations, but she still made sure to let the doctors, nurses, and physical therapists who treated her know about her appreciation and gratitude for curing and caring for her.

She fought a courageous final battle with cancer and made the decision in early May 2012 to return home under my care with the support of hospice. Even during her greatest periods of pain and discomfort, she was more concerned about the well-being of the rest of us.

When the intensity of support started to require 24-hour care, I turned to a local home health agency to supplement the hospice care with a paid personal care attendant. The agency sent over a wonderful aide who bonded closely with my mother during the very first shift.

It gave me comfort to know that I could go and get some needed sleep. After leaving the next morning, I asked my mother how the shift went, and she said the worker was an angel. She spent the entire night at her side, dipping her hands in warm, sudsy water and massaging my mother's entire body with the special moisturizing lotion we had to prevent bedsores. That level of service definitely exceeded my expectations.

I called the home care agency manager later that morning to provide specific positive feedback concerning the worker's high-quality service. When the aide returned the next night for her second scheduled shift, I made sure to provide her directly with the positive feedback I had shared with her manager.

It was nice to learn that the feedback I shared with the manager was passed on to the staff member. She let us know that she and her manager would do the best they could to have her available whenever we needed her. This provided great comfort over the following days.

Not surprisingly, one of my mother's favorite songs was "When You're Smiling" by Larry Shay, Mark Fisher, and Joe Goodwin. The song was made famous by some classic voices such as Duke Ellington, Frank Sinatra, Louis Armstrong, Patti Page, and Nat King Cole.

Whenever I displayed any signs of feeling blue during my childhood, my mother cheerfully sang the song to me. The lyrics are simple and deeply meaningful.

*When you're smiling, When you're smiling, The whole world smiles with you. When you're laughing, When you're laughing, The sun comes shining through. But when you're crying, You bring on the rain. So stop your sighing. Be happy again. Keep on smiling. Cause when you're smiling. The whole world smiles with you.*

My mother energized and motivated everyone who provided support to her. Every doctor, nurse, and nursing assistant loved having my mother as a patient. She brought out the best in everyone by living the song's lyrics every day, including her last. My mother passed away during the early evening on Mother's Day 2012 in the loving arms of my aunt (her dedicated sister) and me.

I realize that not every patient has the contagiously positive attitude of my mother. In fact, a lot of caregivers support loved ones who spend many of their days in a state of anger, depression, pain, and suffering. Under those circumstances, it is easy to be sucked into a state of negative energy that is filled with complaints, despair, and temper tantrums.

If you are caring for a loved one who has an attitude that is challenging to deal with most of the time, it is vital for you to get other skilled and supportive members on your team. Many caregivers in this situation stay on what I call Caregiver Isolation Island. These caregivers may be embarrassed by their loved one's anger, negative attitude, and treatment of others. Or they may be embarrassed by other family dynamics that are filled with trust issues. No matter what—this is one island you want to vote yourself off of as quickly as possible.

The key to transporting yourself far away from Caregiver Isolation Island is to magnetize and motivate skilled and talented specialists to join your support team. Take a little time to analyze and dig deep as to what sources are contributing to the negativity and stress for you and your loved. Once you illuminate the areas of concern, you can identify the human resources to invite on your journey away from Caregiver Isolation Island and toward caregiving without regret.

Here are a few examples of the sources of stress and the associated human resources to help you and your loved one set a clear path to overcoming obstacles of concern.

For physical obstacles such as excessive pain, tiredness, and weakness, ask the treating physician for referrals to other medical or holistic specialists such as an acupuncturist, massage therapist, neurologist, or pain specialist.

For financial concerns such as worry about the ability to afford bills and expenses or concerns about how to invest appropriately to maintain financial security, seek a consultation appointment with a social worker, aging/disability specialist, certified financial planner, or estate planner.

For emotional or spiritual concerns such as depression, loneliness, or questions about the meaning of life and suffering, seek a meeting with your spiritual leader. If you do not associate with a religious or spiritual organization, seek an appointment with a chaplain, counselor, life coach, or reiki practitioner. Another option is to join a support group so you and your loved one can have people in common to share concerns with. Meet with several people and explore different support groups until you find the best fit for you and your loved one.

The above is just a sampling of possible human resources that can help guide you and your loved one into a more positive and purposeful journey. Connect with consultation appointments (often the first ones are free) and let your intuition guide you as to how to maximize the benefits of partnership and performance in new, meaningful relationships.

If you are still uncertain as to which resources to engage, I occasionally offer caregivers free live and practical support to successfully navigate the roadmap to caregiving without regret during a "Caregiving Power Hour" call. When I have them, it's the perfect opportunity for you to bring your concerns and support needs to the call so we can determine which actions and support specialists could be best for you to engage. To get free, on-the-spot, real, practical caregiving solutions, see when the next Caregiving Power Hour is by visiting www.BloomForCoach.com/PowerHour.

This chapter would not be complete if it did not address a key environment that elicits deep concern and fear for caregivers and their loved ones—the hospital. During periods of hospitalization, loved ones very much depend on their caregivers for strong advocacy.

Problems and concerns with treatment arose during the hospitalizations of both of my parents. At times, it was a challenge to remain calm when I was disappointed by the quality of care. The most effective way to deal with concerns is to bring them up right away with a case manager or patient advocate so resolution can be achieved as quickly as possible.

After sharing concerns, make sure to keep the case manager updated with the good aspects of treatment as well as those that can use improvement. Also, make sure to acknowledge and share praise directly with those who are providing it—especially the certified nursing assistants who give such personal care to your loved one.

Even though the healthcare system is becoming increasingly stretched with each passing day, excellence in care is still very attainable. Fortunately, my parents had an excellent primary care team practice. After I started attending all medical appointments with my parents, the primary care physician, nurse practitioner, and nurses all took my input seriously.

Given the extreme challenges that I faced supporting my father after he was struck with vascular dementia, I was relieved that my mother had her full mental capacity and competence right up until her death. One of the greatest challenges that caregivers face is the ability to communicate with medical personnel about their observations of their loved one. Given confidentiality laws and the stubbornness of a loved one when it comes to privacy, important information regarding the patient may fail to get to the physician. After all, the patient is who the appointment is for.

It is understandable that the dialogue during the appointment will mainly occur between the patient and the doctor. A recommended strategy that worked for my mother's care is to negotiate the communication protocol for all appointments.

When we attended appointments, she was the first to answer all of the questions and give direct input. After she was finished, she granted me with permission to provide my observations and concerns with the medical provider during the appointment. This strategy was extremely effective, as it permitted full analysis, communication, and information sharing without defensiveness.

About a year and a half before my mother's passing, my

mother was seriously ill with pneumonia. One of the greatest honors that I received was when the doctor and nurse practitioner shared the opinion that she was safer under my care at home than at a hospital.

Over the course of the next month, we went weekly for appointments to discuss progress. We tried different medications, and my mother made it through the illness. At times, it was very scary. If you have ever heard an elderly person cough and struggle to catch their breath during an episode of pneumonia, it can really rattle you with worry.

During one of the appointments, I shared my fear, so the nurse practitioner actually took the time to call our home at the end of her work day over the next few days to see how things were going. By taking this extra step to provide reassurance, it gave me and my mother the confidence that we could successfully navigate through the storm of pneumonia without hospitalization.

Caregivers are served best when they calmly and clearly communicate with a smile and a bit of sugar. The attitude of gratitude and demonstration of commitment will create an atmosphere that attracts and retains the best team members to join your loved one's care team.

Dig deep and determine the human resources that will enhance the quality of life for both you and your loved one. Maybe it is even time to change certain support personnel for a fresh perspective and new energy. Follow your intuition to select the best resources, and trust in your inner wisdom. Keep evolving and adding specialized components to the care team. This will take you far away from Caregiver Isolation Island and put you firmly on the journey of caregiving without regret.

# Chapter 7 – Access Intuition

Trust your instincts and let your care and dedication guide your decisions.

*"I believe in intuitions and inspirations...*
*I sometimes FEEL that I am right. I do not KNOW that I am."*
~ Albert Einstein

The sixth foundation principle on the road to caregiving without regret is to "access intuition." Families can thrive when caregivers develop and trust this sixth sense for understanding the needs of their loved ones.

Have you ever felt like you had a sixth sense that alerts you to concerns or issues with your loved one? Several times during my journey of care with my parents, I felt this special sixth sense alert me to a serious issue that needed immediate attention and resolution.

Early on during the hospitalization of my father after he was struck by catastrophic heart failure, I had an eerie feeling one morning before leaving to visit him in the hospital. I called his nurse's station to get an update before jumping in the shower to start my morning routine. The nurse on duty reported that he slept most of the night and was actually still sleeping soundly.

After hanging up the phone I took a shower and got dressed but still had this extra sense of concern that something of importance was happening and I needed to be there. Yes, my father had been having a tough time over the previous week. I thought that perhaps I was being overly sensitive given some of the scary events of the prior days.

He had had a pacemaker implanted, which stabilized his heart rate, but his mind was not working like it used to. We were now dealing with dementia, which led to much confusion for him and little understanding as to why he could not go home.

One of the worst events had occurred several days earlier. One evening my father supposedly heard a phone ring outside of his room and got up to answer it. Even though he had a bed alarm on the bed, he managed to walk far enough away before help arrived that he accidentally tore out his catheter.

This awful event led to much more confusion and pain for him and a sinking feeling of despair for me. The good news was that the hospital assigned a 1:1 sitter to my father for the remainder of his hospitalization as a way of avoiding future incidents of injury.

Even though the nurse reported a good overnight and I knew a nice sitter was right by my father's side, I decided to listen to my intuition (gut feeling) and get to the hospital as soon as possible. So, instead of taking time to eat breakfast, I packed a few bagels and a travel mug filled with coffee.

When I arrived at my father's hospital room, he did appear to be sleeping but was very pale. The sitter said to me that he decided to sleep in longer so they let him. When I went over and tried to arouse him, he responded only with a groan. I knew immediately that something was wrong and asked for the nurse to come as soon as possible.

When the nurse came in the room, I informed her that his "sleep" was too heavy and his color was very pale. She checked his vitals and noticed that they had dropped to significantly low levels. Soon after, the doctor was called and my father ended up needing to be moved to intensive care as he was suffering through another troubling cardiovascular event.

Thankfully, I listened to my "gut feeling" that my father needed my help. My intuitive action helped facilitate the attention and care that was needed. As a caregiver, never ignore those heightened concerns that you have for your loved one. Your advocacy and dedication to your loved one's needs could be life-saving.

Intuition is a special gift, so what is it exactly? Intuition can be defined as knowledge gained by the use of the faculty of perceptive insight or a sense of something not evident—an impression.

Some people think that intuition is a special gift that only certain people have. The truth is that we all have intuitive ability. Perhaps you have had experiences that you have not attributed to intuition. Some common intuitive experiences can include:

- Having a hunch about something. You know the best decision to make at the time and it proves to be correct.

- The phone rings and you know who it is before checking the caller ID.

- Noticing a "gut feeling" predicting that something will occur, and it does.

Intuition serves as your own inner mentor. Intuition is readily available and can be accessed consciously when you set aside time to tap into those inner resources. When you take time to let go and ask, your inner intuitive mentor can provide inspired guidance and solutions to your most nagging problems.

One very important caution: do not confuse intuition with your inner critic. Each of us has an inner critic that gives us cautionary messages of things to avoid and worry about. The messaging of the inner critic is based in fear, and attempts to steer us away from certain activities and goals by feeding on our self-doubts that we are not good enough. One common way to know if your inner critic is coming through is when you hear "should statements" in your inner voice (your little voice that speaks to you in your head).

Intuitive abilities can be enhanced when we learn how to transform the fear-based messages of the inner critic into information-based guidance that propels us forward. By doing this, you will transform your inner critic into an inner coach that can provide important nuggets of knowledge to help you make better-informed decisions without keeping you frozen on the bridge to nowhere.

I will share another personal example to illuminate this process. I named my inner critic "worry wart." My inner critic feeds on my fear of not being good enough, taking the form of extreme concern and worry.

I demonstrated this starting as a young child when engaged in complex school assignments. Although I was a conscientious and high-achieving student, I could get consumed with worry about delivering on certain assignments. In fact, my mother used to call me a "worry wart," which is why I chose that name for my inner critic. She always knew how to settle "worry wart" down and soothe my soul with a warm hug, a smile, and one of her fresh-baked chocolate treats.

Once I transformed my inner critic into Coach Worry Wart, he did prove to be a great survival guide during my journey of care. Unfortunately, I did not fully appreciate this skill during my intense experience of in-home caregiving with my father.

At that time, I was consumed with fear-based negative thoughts that caused me to lose tremendous amounts of sleep. After going through coaching certification and training, I learned to pause and listen for the useful information and questions that I was being provided.

Acquiring this skill actually enhanced my intuitive abilities, as I determined the best questions to ask myself in order to regain a sense of calm and control to move forward. It also provided a great vehicle for making the list of questions to ask during medical appointments so I would have as much useful information as I could to provide the best possible care to my mother.

Once you learn how to effectively partner with your inner critic for information and question development, you can be far more open to accessing intuition. Give yourself time to develop this skill by nurturing a relationship with your inner coach. Here are a few ways to access intuition in ways that will enhance your life and safeguard your loved one during the caregiving journey.

First, set aside some quiet time to breathe deeply and go deep into your mind. Yes, this is a form of meditation. Some people do not resonate with meditation, so this strategy may not be for everyone. Don't worry about it. The important idea is to take a few minutes each day to breathe deeply, relax, and center yourself.

Why does deep breathing work so well? When under stress or feeling anxious, many of us tense up and take short breaths. Most of the time, we are not aware of our shallow breathing. Yet when we tense up and limit our breathing in this way, we can sometimes limit the oxygen needed to function properly and without stress. Deep breathing opens things up and drives oxygen throughout the body and brain. As a result, we gain more awareness, energy, information, and an overall sense of well-being.

A fun way to access intuition and calm ourselves can be through doodling. Have a pen and paper with you when you engage in meditation or deep breathing. If you hear words being dictated to you, write them down and allow the words to flow forth freely. If you sense images, draw them, and let your writing hand move effortlessly. Connect the words and images, and just doodle as you feel your hand move naturally.

As you review the words and images, notice how you feel. If you feel calm, you can skip the next paragraph.

If you feel anxiety or fear, pause, close your eyes, and notice what part of your body feels the tension. Don't judge or criticize it. Give attention and love to that part of your body. Imagine what it may look like on the inside. As the image becomes more vivid, notice the colors. Imagine that you are breathing out the colors, and take a few moments to doodle the image on your paper. After you complete the image, pause and study the image. What do you see in the image? What feelings emerge as you study the image? Try to give the image a title and write it down on the paper. Your image is neither good nor bad. It just represents what you are experiencing in this moment in your core. Bringing the image forth and onto the paper will help take the stress and worry out of your inner self.

Take a break and refresh yourself with a glass of water. Once you are in a state of calm, study the words and images on your paper again. Most of the time, valuable insight and knowledge can be gained from this connection to your inner self. The wonderful aspect of this exercise is that you can forge this gateway to accessing your intuition in less than ten minutes. And it is free other than the cost of a piece of paper and some crayons or colored markers.

As you engage in the simple activities described above, you will find that intuition will surface more freely, and when you least expect it. More importantly, you will be taking this brief and valuable time to center yourself and focus on self-care.

Intuition serves as a needed and welcomed guide for survival and success along the caregiving journey. Once you open this gateway to intuition, trust your instincts and let your care and dedication for your loved one guide your decisions.

# Chapter 8 –
# Put Chocolate in Your Pillbox

Reward yourself to fuel your soul so you can thrive during the long journey as a caregiver and develop the passion and purpose for your life beyond caregiving.

*"Nourishing yourself in a way that helps you blossom in the direction you want to go is attainable, and you are worth the effort."*
~ Deborah Day

The final foundation principle on the road to caregiving without regret is to "put chocolate in your pillbox." You may be chuckling a bit right now, which is the usual reaction I receive when I share this principle in live, energizing caregiver workshops and pass around a basket of chocolate candy.

Once again, let me be clear that I do not have a bias against prescription medications. In fact, I believe that it is vital that caregivers work in close consultation with their physicians to develop a preventative health and wellness plan that may include some prescription medications. After all, the most serious risk to a loved one receiving care is the serious illness, hospitalization, or death of the primary caregiver.

The good news is that caregivers generally follow through with doctors' orders to avoid illness by taking their medicines as prescribed. In order to avoid cavities and tooth decay, people follow daily routines of tooth brushing that become second nature.

Consistent follow-through with hygiene and medication routines is of primary importance for maintaining health and wellness. Yet caregivers remain highly susceptible to depression and physical illness because they rarely provide themselves with rewards that develop the passion and purpose for their life beyond caregiving. By determining their special "chocolate" (which is a metaphor for something that provides joy, laughter, and satisfaction) and dosing themselves regularly, family caregivers will create enduring satisfaction and success as a matter of sacred and essential routine.

So what is your special chocolate? How do you determine what your special chocolate is?

Think back to your life before you began your role as a family caregiver. What types of leisure and recreational activities did you enjoy? Make a list. See what brings an extra skip to your heart, a smile to your face, or a little twinge of excitement when you think of it.

Some of these enjoyable activities can go far back in your life. One former client discussed how she used to enjoy singing in her high school chorus. She had always enjoyed singing but had never pursued it as a passion beyond high school. As she put it: "Life happened." She landed a job, a husband, and two children.

One of her children was born with special needs associated with developmental disabilities. She engaged in a lifelong commitment to this child, and her husband has been in recent need of her care after suffering a stroke a few years ago.

After my inquiry about what brought her so much joy

from the chorus, she said it was the friendships and the excitement of performing. She set an intention during the session to explore group singing lessons or a local choir to join. She ended up doing both, which became part of her weekly routine within a few months of that session.

She discovered and indulged in her special chocolate on a regular basis. It was very satisfying, and calorie-free. By taking this special time for herself each week, she began the process of living her own life more fully—which is the most important ingredient to caregiving without regret.

What are some activities that you have enjoyed or would like to bring back into your life? Here are some categories and activities for consideration as you do some self-exploration.

If you enjoy music, you may want to participate or take lessons in singing, composing, learning how to play an instrument, downloading favorite songs, or attending concerts. I actually have an uncle, one of my mother's younger brothers, who decided at the age of 75 to learn how to play the harp. He committed to lessons and actually gave a concert a year after starting his lessons. I have joked with him that he has learned to play the harp in preparation for giving amazing concerts on a cloud once he earns his angel wings. The bottom line is that you are never too old to explore or learn how to do a new activity such as playing an instrument.

If you enjoy dancing, you may want to participate or take lessons in folk dancing, square dancing, aerobics, ballet, tap, line dancing, or zumba. A good friend and colleague who served as her husband's primary caregiver during his courageous battle with cancer took up tango as a hobby. This dancing interest has grown to the point that she frequently partners with other excellent dancers in a variety of public settings. She has even purchased some amazing tango dance costumes and frequently shares her dancing moves through pictures on social media. It is so inspiring to see how far she has come with her hobby and to see that it serves as her special chocolate to keep her moving forward with energy in her life beyond caregiving.

If you enjoy arts and crafts, you may want to participate or take lessons in drawing, knitting, sewing, painting, crocheting, embroidery, weaving, ceramics, glass blowing, pottery, jewelry making, photography, baking, or cooking. A former caregiver client enjoyed crafts and used the talents she developed during her caregiving journey to make holiday gifts for her friends and family members. The gift recipients treasured her handmade special crafts (her latest one was a set of handmade scented soaps), and she found peace and relaxation while working on the projects. Another added benefit—her own family did not need to purchase any hand or bath soaps during the next year.

If you enjoy table games, you may want to participate in or form a weekly game night. Some favorite games may include: cards, checkers, chess, bingo, scrabble, monopoly, dominoes, or other common favorites. Many games now can be played over popular video gaming systems with multiple players. Games or puzzles can also serve as an enjoyable, relaxing, and brain stimulating 1:1 activities for caregivers and their loved ones. My 91-year-old aunt loves to complete puzzles. When any of her children, grandchildren, or nephews comes for a visit, it is natural to join her in completing one of her puzzles over a nice cup of tea.

If you enjoy outdoor leisure and recreational activities,

you may want to participate in or take lessons in hiking, rock climbing, camping, gardening, fishing, canoeing, bicycling, skiing, ice skating, rollerblading, bird watching, golfing, tennis, soccer, swimming, or scuba diving. Your local YMCA or other social clubs can offer many opportunities to try new activities. This can be a great way to rekindle old friendships or meet new people while getting fresh air and exercise in an enjoyable way.

If you are fulfilled by providing community service and volunteer support, you may want to participate in a food bank, homeless shelter, political campaign, Special Olympics, community cleanup, community gardening, or as a committee member in a religious, social, or nonprofit agency. These volunteer opportunities provide great ways to meet new people who are like-minded and may be available to provide some support to you in your caregiving situation.

If you enjoy continuing education and research, contact local community colleges or other educational institutions for class offerings. There are also many group learning opportunities via the Internet that can provide you with intellectual stimulation and support from the comfort and convenience of your own home.

The bottom line is that there are many opportunities within reach for you to explore old and new interests. Give the gift of attention and time for yourself. Find your special chocolate and dose yourself regularly. Share your passion with others and find support so you can take the time to do the things that you enjoy. You are an inspirational caregiver, and you deserve it!

It is important to point out that the activities and rewards that you give yourself will not only fuel your soul so you can thrive during your journey as a caregiver, they will develop the passion and purpose for your life beyond caregiving. When the day comes that you no longer serve as a caregiver, you will be grateful that you have other parts of your life and a social support network to tap into.

# Chapter 9 –
# Life Beyond Caregiving

What happens after your caregiving journey comes to an end?

*"Nothing is so awesomely unfamiliar as the familiar that discloses itself at the end of a journey."*

~ Cynthia Ozick

Sadly, the caregiving journey usually comes to an end when our loved one passes away as a result of aging, illness, or disease. As with life, each of our experiences with grief and loss is a unique and personal journey.

For some, the passing of the loved one may bring an initial sense of comfort and relief in the knowledge that the pain and suffering is over. Others may immediately enter a state of disbelief while experiencing numbness and shock that the loved one has passed away. Some survivors enter the mourning and bereavement period with a feeling of profound loss and sadness that no amount of comfort can relieve.

Mourning can be described as the public rituals or symbols for bereavement that occur during the initial days after the death of a loved one. During this period, depending upon one's cultural or faith background, there is typically a funeral or memorial service and public expressions of loss, love, and support for the surviving family members. The period of mourning is usually time-limited, and within a few days everyone returns to their normal routines. Meanwhile, the bereaved caregiver can often feel lost and alone as the journey of grief is just beginning, which can understandably take most people several months or years to work through.

As with every journey of care, every journey of grief is unique. There is no magic bullet, pill, or prescription for easing or erasing feelings associated with grief. And there is no appropriate or set timeline for experiencing the stages of grief. It is important to not suppress feelings of sadness and pass through the stages and storms of grief one day at a time.

The journey of grief can be long and rough. Caregivers tend to be focused squarely on the needs of their loved ones while paying very little attention to their own needs during the caregiving journey. It is no wonder that the responsibilities of caregiving consume the caregiver's life and can eventually erode their identity and leave them at a loss when the loved one is no longer in their care. After the passing of a loved one, the caregiver's daily habits and routine become severely disrupted.

I can remember this state vividly several days after my mother's funeral when the last of the out-of-town relatives returned home. The first morning that I was alone in the house was difficult. After waking up, I moved on autopilot, started the coffee maker, and set two plates and cups at the dining table for breakfast. Once I realized that my mother was no longer there and that I just needed to make breakfast for one, I burst into tears and lost my appetite.

The passing of the loved one puts the caregiver in an uncomfortable and unfamiliar position of re-establishing their own needs and identity. Not only does the caregiver grieve for the loss of their loved one, but they also grieve for the loss of their caregiver identity, a role that may have been in existence for many years. During the initial period after the loss of a loved one, it is important for family caregivers to reconnect with their own identities and reground their spirits before making any important, life-changing decisions.

Friends and family members are very likely to offer support and unsolicited advice. Caregivers, who are very vulnerable at this time, may be tempted to make unsound decisions that they may regret later on. It is helpful for the caregiver to have someone they can trust by their side who can help the caregiver deal with individuals who push ideas that may overwhelm them in their exhausted and saddened state.

Although there is no way to fully prepare and immediately experience joy as one creates a new life beyond caregiving, there are things that can be done to make the transition a bit smoother. It is important to discuss and plan with loved ones when they can still make decisions about their desires for what they want to happen after they pass away. Pre-planning for funeral and memorial services can be a godsend for the bereaved caregiver, who will likely be extremely stressed and sleep deprived immediately after the passing of their loved one.

I was greatly relieved that my father had worked with an estate planning attorney and funeral director to line up all contracts and documents several years prior to his catastrophic heart failure event. In fact, my parents and I worked together on this process while everyone was still fairly healthy and

definitely of sound mind. There were several amazing benefits of this pre-planning that helped me navigate through the
financial and legal obligations throughout the journey of care
and beyond.

By working with an estate attorney, all documents were in
place so that I could serve as a health care proxy and power
of attorney when both of my parents could no longer speak
for themselves. This allowed me to easily work closely with
all medical personnel and take care of household financial
responsibilities by having easy access to their accounts for
bill paying. In addition, the estate plan that was put in place
allowed for a seamless transition of turning over assets to my
parents' beneficiaries without spending tremendous amounts
of time and money going through probate court.

By working with a funeral director to develop pre-planned
funeral arrangements, everything was in place according to
my parents' wishes. At the time of each parent's passing, the
hospice nurse was able to call a phone number to the funeral
home, and within an hour the bodies were honorably trans-
ported and the pre-planned arrangements took over. The only
thing I had to do was to coordinate the day and time for the
funerals and send over a set of clothes for burial. I could not
imagine having to go through the process of selecting coffins,
discussing all details of the arrangements, and anxiously considering costs, immediately after traveling through the very
painful and exhausting period of supporting my loved one's
end-of-life journey.

I am truly grateful that both of my parents were able to
age in place and die with dignity in the comfort of their
home. My father passed away in December of 2009 and my
mother on Mother's Day 2012—both in my loving arms as

they drew their last breaths. This was made possible because I partnered with wonderful hospice teams.

Many people do not engage hospice until the final days or even hours of a loved one's life. Hospice is a service that can be engaged if someone has a life expectancy of six months or less. Almost every insurance plan covers 100% of hospice benefits, and hospice can also be used in group community settings or nursing homes as well as private homes. Besides providing incredible medical, physical, and spiritual support to the loved one in care, hospice provides needed and welcomed support to caregivers and other surviving family members.

This support also continues after the death of the loved one through grief counseling services. The bereavement support counselors and support groups offered by my parents' hospice agencies have been such an important source of support to me during my grief journey. Even if your loved one did not use hospice services, many local hospice organizations offer free grief support workshops to members of the public.

If you have not yet experienced the passing of your loved one, it is recommended that you begin to discuss and plan for the end-of-life journey. These discussions can be difficult, but they are very necessary for each and every one of us. Unless someone makes a discovery of the fountain of immortality, end-of-life planning is necessary. As a caregiver, this is one of the rare opportunities that you have to bring a sense of control and order into your life.

It is also highly recommended that you identify and pursue interests that will sustain you as you transition to a new life beyond caregiving. Some activities that you enjoyed prior to caregiving may seem foreign, uncomfortable, or unfamiliar after the passing of your loved one.

As shared in the previous chapter, this is why it is so important to "put chocolate in your pillbox" during your journey of care as a matter of sacred and essential routine so these enjoyable activities are familiar and enjoyed by you. By dosing yourself with regularly scheduled activities, you can have goals and a sense of purpose when you no longer serve as a caregiver. So take focused time to determine your special chocolate and engage in those activities of growth, development, and joy so you can more readily move forward in your life beyond caregiving.

After my father passed away, I was determined (with my mother's support) to pursue interests outside of my caregiving role. I completed coaching certification and training, volunteered on nonprofit boards of directors, became an active member of my religious community, started coaching fellow caregivers, and even traveled occasionally for personal development retreats. I have a vast network of friends and colleagues who have supported and sustained me as I seek to move forward and recalibrate my life beyond caregiving.

I will not sugar-coat this journey. Even with my best efforts, it has not been easy. There are days that I feel lost, lonely, and depressed. On those days, I just want to stay in bed and under the covers and cry over a box of chocolates. I lovingly allow myself to experience those down times when I need to. I choose not to stay there day after day by consciously deciding to engage in an enjoyable activity or by contacting a friend or my bereavement counselor for support when I need it.

During the first year after the passing of a loved one, there are the painful first anniversaries that pass. You go through the first birthdays, holiday season, wedding anniversaries, father's day, mother's day, and day of death. You may be told that the first of each of these anniversary dates are the toughest. That may indeed be true for you.

For others, it might be the second, third, or even tenth years. Again, there is no right or wrong for feelings of grief. Accept yourself for who you are and your unique experience. The storms of grief come and go. Do not fight or try to avoid the storms—pass through them with cleansing tears if you need to. The loss of a loved one is profound and painful. If you are sad, it is because they meant so much to you.

One of the greatest pieces of advice I have received from my bereavement counselor is to create new traditions and find ways to honor your loved one on the anniversary days with people who support you. Sadness and tears may be part of these experiences, as well as memories filled with laughter.

After the passing of your loved one, you see and experience life through a new lens. Although it can seem really difficult at times, try to create or chart a new course and honor your loved one's legacy by moving forward with your own life.

You have provided much love and support as a dedicated caregiver, and you are so deserving of all the beauty and gifts life has to bring as you travel through it. After all, your loved one would want you to live your life to the fullest.

# Chapter 10 –
# Take Inspired Action

Go forth as an energetic caregiver living without regret.

*"Accept yourself. Love yourself as you are. Your finest work, your best movements, your joy, peace, and healing comes when you love yourself. You give a great gift to the world when you do that. You give others permission to do the same: to love themselves. Revel in self-love. Roll in it. Bask in it as you would sunshine."*

~ Melody Beattie

Congratulations on taking the time for *you* to study this survival guide for caregiving without regret! While you likely entered your role as a family caregiver accidentally as a result of an unexpected accident, illness, disease, or disability of your loved one, you stay in the role as a dedicated caregiver by choice.

You have the power each and every day to start with a clean slate and set the intention to complete one small activity or step that benefits your health and well-being. Self-care is not selfish! It actually fosters your ability to support your loved one for the long-term.

This book contains many practical and tactical coping strategies to inspire you to provide care without regret. You have explored the roadmap to: confidently navigate through periods of crisis, stop feeling like a victim of circumstances, overcome conflict and family dynamics, achieve buy-in, lead your family and friends to contribute in meaningful ways, attract and retain the best expertise and talent, access your intuition, and create a rewarding life for yourself while serving as an inspiring caregiver and beyond.

If you admire and focus on your contributions and stop dwelling on your perceived shortcomings, you will more easily move forward fully with other goals and activities in your life. This will be especially beneficial when your caregiving journey comes to an end and you transition to a life without your loved one.

If you have read this book and feel a bit overwhelmed with implementing all of the foundational principles and associated tips, that is normal and understandable. Once you have read the entire book, choose one tip that really resonates with you and implement it.

You do not need to progress through the roadmap in a linear way from start to finish. In fact, all caregivers bounce around the roadmap. Ideally, you want to familiarize yourself with all of the foundation principles so you can use them in perfect timing during your caregiving journey. Once you master them, you will be able to repeat them with greater ease.

Start with one baby step from anywhere along the roadmap that you can complete quickly. Take imperfect and inspired action. Don't hold yourself back due to your fear or desire for perfection—just do it! This will build momentum to take the next step.

Life is fragile, and every moment is temporary. Hopelessness is a mindset that can be transformed. If you feel overworked, completely drained, and drowning in the responsibilities of having someone's life in your hands day in and day out, remember that you are not alone.

Have faith that you are resilient and can experience some well-earned relief. You can renew your personal energy so you can choose to be a source of unconditional love and support for the long term. After all, you are a caregiver. Caregivers deserve admiration and respect as members of the greatest force for safeguarding the well-being of the most vulnerable in society. I am proud to count you among this treasured caring force.

Go forth with energy and care, fellow caregiver!

# Appendix A –
# Frequently Asked Questions

## For the Times You May Need
## Emergency Roadside Assistance
## During Your Caregiving Journey

*"Any knowledge that doesn't lead to new questions*
*quickly dies out: it fails to maintain the temperature*
*required for sustaining life."*

~ Wislawa Szymborska

Some frequently asked questions that emerge after reading this book may include the following.

**Question:** *Many of the tips and suggestions sound really nice and potentially helpful. Yet I can barely get everything done each day now. Time is just whipping by and I fail to manage it. How can I find the time to do all or any of this?*

**Answer:** This is the most common complaint of caregivers. I don't have time. The truth is you do and there are parts of each day you can choose to take for yourself. The key is to choose one activity in this book and take one baby step toward accomplishing it. Start small and build momentum. Acknowledge and celebrate your success, no matter how tiny it seems. Then, keep moving on your journey to caregiving without regret, one inspired step at a time.

**Question:** *The person I care for is so grumpy and negative every day. Every action I take leads to complaining and whining. I am feeling sad and weighed down most of the time. I want to support my loved one, but what do I do if I really do not like this person?*

**Answer:** It is not uncommon to love, yet not like, the family member that you are caring for. This really goes back to acceptance. Give yourself permission to accept who you are and who the person you care for is. We are each unique. You make a choice each and every day to be a caregiver. You really do not have to do it—nursing homes and other care organizations are available.

If you are determined to stick it out, add a key human resource to your support team to help you and your family member communicate more effectively and respectfully. Get off Caregiver Isolation Island. Note that if you have some very deep issues from the way you were raised or how you are currently being treated, you should make an appointment with a coach or therapist and seek help.

**Question:** *What if my usually nice parent or loved one starts behaving badly? Sometimes I am bearing the brunt of name-calling and other verbal outbursts. At times, my loved one is refusing to eat or take medications. The uncharacteristic anger and stubbornness is really getting under my skin.*

**Answer:** This is probably one of the most difficult aspects of caregiving to deal with and is especially common when families are touched by Alzheimer's disease or dementia. After my father was struck with vascular dementia and lost all short-term memory, I dealt with the challenges associated with his temper tantrums that were directly linked to his confusion.

Prior to his illness my father operated in a very calm, logical, and predictable way—he was a chemist, and organization was extremely important to him. Once struck by dementia, he would request to go home (while sitting in his living room) as the sun went down. This phenomenon of confusion is actually called "sun-downing."

The other time of day that led to confusion was when he woke up around 3 or 4 a.m. most nights and got dressed to take the train to school (something he did decades earlier when he attended college). In order to survive these moments of confusion and not worry about my father leaving the house overnight in the freezing cold to seek a nearby train stop that did not exist, I would get up with him and prepare him a breakfast before he left for school. Once he got through the meal, he typically forgot that he wanted to leave and would go to a comfortable chair in front of the television and would start dozing. At about 8 a.m., he would join my mother and me for a second breakfast and we would go about the day.

Even with my best efforts, there were times when I was unable to navigate peacefully through my father's confusion. This would lead to his yelling and very uncharacteristic name-calling. The key to surviving those hurtful and heart-wrenching moments was to remember how much love, respect, and support my father had always shown me. It was very sad that the person I was dealing with was a shell of who my father used to be. Fortunately, I was able to take comfort in the moments when he looked at me with a smile. During those special caregiving moments, I knew that the man I had loved and looked up to my entire life was somewhere deep inside that fog of confusion.

**Question:** *I feel as though I spend a lot of time on the phone updating friends and family members. When they offer to help, I always say I have it covered. I don't know what to ask for. How can I be more efficient with communication and get support when I need it?*

**Answer:** It is nice to have a lot of people who want to check in and get updates, but it can definitely be draining to repeat the same story over and over again. There are simple resources available for lining up desired support and delivering information to a number of parties efficiently. For caregivers who enjoy using the Internet, free, easy-to-navigate systems to build support networks can be found at www.LotsaHelpingHands.com or the family portal at www.SeniorCareSociety.com.

Through these online communities, family caregivers can post vital medical and support information, use an online calendar to schedule volunteer assistance for activities/appointments, and send updates with just the click of a button. These tools greatly simplify the organizational process and provide a journaling vehicle for you to share key points along the caregiving journey. If we spoke, I could probably give you more specific ideas.

**Question:** *What if I do not use the Internet? How can I get the information and support that I need in a world that seems to be moving beyond me?*

**Answer:** Old-school options such as calendars, post-it-notes, and dry erase boards are just as effective. Create an information binder for family, friends, and volunteers so vital medical and support needs are at their fingertips. Houses of worship, service providers, or local volunteer organizations can be of assistance to building a super helpful and responsive support community for your family.

To share information to keep all the key family members and friends in the know, assign one specific person to be your spokesperson or sharer of information. After a grueling and long day of appointments, medical tests, and treatment, you may feel too exhausted to have to call a long list of people for updates. By having a point person for this communication role, you can share the vital details with him or her and let that person complete the rounds of calls or e-mail updates.

***Question:*** *What other documents and resources are beneficial for caregivers and loved ones to consider for effective care planning?*

**Answer:** Some documents to consider when talking about planning are: the durable power of attorney (for managing financial and practical affairs when one is not capable), the healthcare proxy or power of attorney (for assignment of parties to make medical decisions when one is not capable), and a living will (advance care directives that provide detailed instructions for health care proxies to follow when faced with certain treatment or end-of-life care decisions and options).

Check with your local, state, or provincial websites for appropriate eldercare documents and information. These sites may have legally accepted copies that can be downloaded, printed, and signed for free. For more complex issues and guidance, consult with an eldercare or estate planning attorney about these and other necessary documents, such as a will or revocable living trust that may be needed for your situation. An experienced attorney can guide you through understanding your options and drafting documents to best meet your needs.

***Question:*** *What if my loved one refuses to discuss issues related to effective care planning and end of life issues?*

**Answer:** This is one of the most challenging situations to discuss. Before engaging in the full details involved in the discussion, let your loved one know how important it is for you to clearly understand their preferences and wishes if the time comes that they cannot speak for themselves. This will validate them to let them know you care. Express your understanding that completing these documents can be uncomfortable and worrisome.

You may even want to consider completing a set for yourself. After all, we can become incapacitated at any time and at any age. Having documents lined up in advance will make it much easier for those left behind to make decisions. By setting a time to complete forms together, you will demonstrate the importance of completing these documents for everyone, and this daunting and scary task is much more likely to get completed.

If you understandably still have trouble getting started with these forms and completing a health care proxy, I am skilled at facilitating the completion of these forms. I have helped a number of people determine their end-of-life wishes in a safe and comfortable way—just reach out if you would like support.

**Question:** *My loved one has been given a troubling prognosis and is not expected to live much longer. I have learned that we could start hospice support at any time. My loved one thinks it is a death sentence and wants to keep fighting. I have mixed feelings and wonder how soon to get hospice in place. How do I make this decision and what does hospice support offer?*

**Answer:** This is one of the most frightening decisions that anyone ever has to make. It is not time for hospice if your loved one is currently benefiting from treatments intended to cure their illness. For some terminally ill patients, though, there comes a point when treatment is no longer working. Continued attempts at treatment may even be harmful, or in some cases treatment might provide another few weeks or months of life, but will make your loved one feel too ill to enjoy much of that time. While hope for a full recovery may be gone, there is still hope for as much quality time as possible to spend with loved ones, as well as hope for a dignified and pain-free death.

If a doctor has certified your loved one's prognosis as not longer than six months, she/he is eligible for hospice. This applies to anyone of any age, with any type of illness. People with Alzheimer's are usually referred to hospice when they are in the final stages of the illness, which can be very helpful to family members even if the person can no longer communicate.

If your loved one is competent and capable of making decisions, allow them to express their personal wisdom with this choice. One way to encourage a person to make a decision to accept hospice services is to let them know that it is not irreversible. In fact, there are many stories of people improving and living longer as a result of receiving hospice services. One can self-discharge from hospice at any time, and services can be restarted again at a later date.

Hospice services are extremely helpful for families, as all insurance policies typically pick up 100% of hospice charges. Services can include the delivery of medication and medical supplies directly to the home, visits by nurses and personal care assistants, light housekeeping such as laundry, twenty-four-hour on-call support, and bereavement support for family members. Hospice agencies often have community outreach nurses and workers who can be available to educate you and your loved one about the benefits and services of hospice or other bridge support options such as palliative care.

**Question:** *I am turning to friends and other family for support. I hate to be dependent on others. How can I get over this feeling and the worry that others may think that I am taking advantage of them without anything in return?*

**Answer:** Many caregivers have a few of these concerns run through their minds at times. For the most part, people will be glad to support you and your loved one without expectation of "payback." Sometimes, the greatest reward you can give someone is the expression of gratitude. Another possibility is to think of your own talents. You could exchange or barter a talent or product for the caregiving support you receive. You might be surprised to learn what others might appreciate from you that you could enjoy providing. Perhaps it is one of my favorites—a yummy fresh-baked chocolate treat.

*Question:* *After my loved one passes away, where can I turn for support to help me through the process of grief and transition to my role beyond caregiving?*

Answer: If your loved one used hospice services, surviving family members can access direct bereavement support from the agency for up to a year after the loved one's death. Agencies typically have licensed social workers and therapists who can provide 1:1 and group grief counseling support.

The support received from hospice agencies has been personally helpful after the loss of each of my parents. Even if your loved one did not use hospice support, many hospice organizations host group bereavement support sessions that are free and open to the public.

Besides counseling, many life coaches are now specializing in grief and how to support the development of goals to keep moving clients forward through the storms along the grief journey. After the loss of your loved one, you may feel that you are losing a strong part of your identity as a caregiver. This is normal. Even if the responsibilities were difficult, there can be a let-down with the loss of such a key life role.

Set aside time to talk to professionals and trusted family members or friends who will fully listen to you as you process through memories and share your thoughts. Giving yourself the time and space to journey through grief is instrumental to healing and renewal. Seek support during this journey—do not travel alone to Post-Caregiving Isolation Island.

If you have additional burning questions, reach out for assistance. One of the bonuses for purchasing this book is the ability to take a *free* Caregiving Burnout Risk Assessment and to schedule a *free* Caregiving Recharge Session. Your concerns, ideas, and questions about any topic can be explored during this session. Go to www.BurnoutRisk.com for more information. Do not delay—access your free assessment and bonuses now!

Energetically yours,

Michael